HOW CAN I
FEEL PRODUCTIVE
AS A MOM?

✘ Cultivating Biblical Godliness

Series Editors

Joel R. Beeke and Ryan M. McGraw

Dr. D. Martyn Lloyd-Jones once said that what the church needs to do most of all is "to begin herself to live the Christian life. If she did that, men and women would be crowding into our buildings. They would say, 'What is the secret of this?'" As Christians, one of our greatest needs is for the Spirit of God to cultivate biblical godliness in us in order to put the beauty of Christ on display through us, all to the glory of the triune God. With this goal in mind, this series of booklets treats matters vital to Christian experience at a basic level. Each booklet addresses a specific question in order to inform the mind, warm the affections, and transform the whole person by the Spirit's grace, so that the church may adorn the doctrine of God our Savior in all things.

HOW CAN I
FEEL PRODUCTIVE
AS A MOM?

ESTHER ENGELSMA

REFORMATION HERITAGE BOOKS
GRAND RAPIDS, MICHIGAN

How Can I Feel Productive as a Mom?
© 2017 by Esther Engelsma

Reformation Heritage Books
3070 29th St. SE
Grand Rapids, MI 49512
616-977-0889
orders@heritagebooks.org
www.heritagebooks.org

Printed in the United States of America
22 23 24 25 26/10 9 8 7 6 5 4 3 2

ISBN 978-1-60178-584-8
ISBN 978-1-60178-585-5 (e-pub)

For additional Reformed literature, request a free book list from Reformation Heritage Books at the above regular or e-mail address.

HOW CAN I
FEEL PRODUCTIVE
AS A MOM?

———— ✳ ————

Sitting at my mom's kitchen table with my baby in my arms and tears in my eyes, I shared for the first time how unproductive the work of motherhood and homemaking felt. It broke my heart to admit it because I knew the work was meaningful. Even as I sat there, my mom reminded me of the value of raising children and influencing their souls. I knew that I must be getting things done because my baby was content and my house was fairly clean, but I could not seem to feel productive at the end of the day. My favorite days had always been the ones when I checked the most tasks off my list, but now the tasks didn't stay checked off. They had to be done over and over, and there were so many, and I could never figure out if I should be cooking, cleaning, playing, working, snuggling, relaxing, or sleeping. No matter which I chose, I felt like I should have used my time for something better. Would I ever feel productive as a mom?

A year later, my answer is yes, not because I get more done than I did then but because God has used His Word to change the way I think about my work. I thought that God's call to us, God's will for us, and God's purpose in creating us all centered on getting things done. They don't.

- God's call to you is not to get things done but to use time well.

- God's will for you is not to get things done but to grow in sanctification.

- God's purpose in creating you is not to get things done but to glorify Him.

Getting things done is part of using time well. Using time well is part of growing in sanctification. Growing in sanctification is part of glorifying God. The end of it all is to glorify God. The most basic tool is getting things done, or productivity. The tool is meant to be used but not idolized. It is a means; it is not an end. Because it is only a means, we will never be satisfied when we make it our end.

GET THINGS DONE

Have you ever stopped to think about what your end goal of mothering really is? Isn't it to show your children Jesus, to shape their minds so that when God is ready to work in their lives they are ready to believe? What you really want to "get done" is whatever will lead to the salvation and sanctification of your family.

Yet strangely, most of our thoughts and conversations revolve around laundry and cleaning and feeding mouths rather than feeding souls. There is a place for all that, but our minds should be dominated by loftier thoughts about God and about how to point our family's souls to the one thing needed! We must take "the long view of motherhood" which "sees far beyond the third trimester, potty training, and even high school graduation. The long view of motherhood scans the horizon of eternity."[1]

But daily productivity is important to this long view because it is a tool to help you focus on and further your goal of the salvation and sanctification of your family—a goal only God can achieve and yet a goal He has called you to work toward (Prov. 22:6). Spiritual success is never up to you, yet you must bring the gospel to your children. God is the only one who can give the fruit, yet you are called to obedience and faithfulness. Getting things done is necessary so that you can keep your eyes on eternity. It's hard to find time to talk to your children about Jesus when you've been procrastinating on other things. It's hard to be an example of devotion when you rarely put down your phone to take up your Bible. A Christian who is living in obedience to God is a Christian who gets things done because the work is given by God.

---

1. Gloria Furman, *Treasuring Christ When Your Hands Are Full: Gospel Meditations for Busy Moms* (Wheaton, Ill.: Crossway, 2014), 153.

But even obedience and faithfulness in our work don't guarantee we will feel productive because motherhood is not efficient work—at least not in the way you and I think of efficiency. The beauty is that Jesus's life was not "efficient" either. He came into the world as a baby and had to learn everything from scratch—crawling, standing, walking, and talking. He didn't start His ministry until He was thirty, and then He "only" ministered for three years. He spent a lot of time with a few people who didn't seem to understand what He was trying to teach them. Some days He healed crowds of people; other days He went into the wilderness alone. He washed feet, served meals, and gave up His life.

If I had been in control of Jesus's ministry, I feel sure I could have planned it more efficiently. I would have gathered massive groups of people so His words could impact them all at once. Doesn't it seem like a waste that so many lessons were taught to just twelve men? I would have made sure that every time He healed, all the sick people would be gathered in one spot so that He could heal them all at once. I would have put Him into the world as a thirty-year-old so that He could be wise and mature immediately. I would have had Him minister for forty years or more. I would have assumed that since Jesus *is* God, He wouldn't need any time to talk *to* His Father. There are so many ways I could have made His time on earth more "efficient." Elisabeth Elliot says,

How many "if only's" He must have left behind, how much more that He "could have" done.... Still He was able to make that amazing claim, "I have finished the work You gave me to do." This was not the same as saying He had finished everything He could possibly think of to do or that He had done everything others had asked. He made no claim to have done what He wanted to do. The claim was that He had done what had been *given*.[2]

Do you catch yourself telling God how much you could get done for Him if only your children would stop fighting or take longer naps? Do you struggle with how long it takes to feed a baby? Do you question the value of all your time spent washing bodies and serving meals? Do you wonder why God designed mothering to require putting so much time and energy into influencing so few people? Do you feel you are wasting your potential? Wouldn't you be more useful if you had great influence over many people?

These are the questions I struggled with, and I still don't have answers. I never would have chosen discipleship as the core of Jesus's ministry or of motherhood. But God did, and we don't have to understand why. He doesn't expect that of us, just as we don't expect our toddlers to understand all the

---

2. Elisabeth Elliot, *Discipline: The Glad Surrender* (Grand Rapids: Revell, 1982), 99.

reasons we put peas on their plates. But we do have to trust that His way is better and His thoughts are higher than ours. We have to trust that what God says is effective is better than what we think is efficient. And in trusting, we have to obey, just as we expect our toddlers to obey by eating their peas.

Trusting that this "inefficient" method is God's chosen way gives peace when you can't make everything in motherhood as efficient as you would like it to be. It can be hard to get used to and to accept that tasks will take more time than they did before. There will be interruptions and messes and days when the baby doesn't nap, and you will need to remind yourself again and again that these things are not keeping you from your work. They are your work—work given to you by a good God whose thoughts and ways are far above yours.

Does this mean you shouldn't strive for productivity and efficiency within your work? Of course not. With time, practice, and Google, you can get better and faster at the tasks of mothering and homemaking. But never let getting things done be your main goal or get in the way of your main goal. Productivity and efficiency are merely God-given tools to help you push toward your ultimate goal of the salvation and sanctification of your family.

USE TIME WELL

While we may understand that productivity and efficiency are merely tools for the Christian mother and not her main purpose on earth, we live in a culture that is obsessed with Getting Things Done, and it can be difficult to separate ourselves from it. We live like modern-day Marthas in a distracted, anxious, troubled whirlwind of activity, always reaching for new apps, planners, checklists, printables, blogs, workbooks, and systems that are rumored to hold *the* key to unlocking the perfect balance of peace and productivity.

Yet nowhere in the Bible are we called to get as much done as possible. Instead, we are told to redeem the time, or to make the best use of time (Eph. 5:16). Redeeming the time, explained seventeenth-century theologian Matthew Poole, is "a metaphor taken from merchants, that diligently observe the time for buying and selling, and easily part with their pleasure for gain."[3] With an almost endless array of items to buy, a good merchant would use his knowledge and experience to purchase the things that would make the best use of his money. His decision would depend on many factors, including the amount of money he had, the time of day, and the season. He made a logical business decision, not an emotional one. He was in control of his money.

To redeem your time, follow the example of the good merchant. Imagine your time as currency. Every day you are given twenty-four hours.

---

3. Matthew Poole, *A Commentary on the Holy Bible*, vol. 3 (London: Banner of Truth, 1969), 3:676, commentary on Eph. 5:16.

In order to do something, you pay out an amount of time. Your decision about what to do with your next stretch of time—whether it is five minutes or two hours—will be based on many different factors, including how much time you have, how much energy you have, whether your kids are awake or sleeping, and whether there are urgent needs to be met. Based on these factors, you figure out what to do right now to make the best use of your time. Your decision is logical, not emotional. You are the master of your time, not the servant. Your time does not control you. You control it.

What, exactly, does it mean to use time well? Simply that you are doing what you should be doing when you should be doing it. Before you became a mom, using time well almost always led to checking many tasks off your list. As a mom, though, using time well doesn't guarantee that you will get everything, or even anything, checked off your list. Children have a way of interrupting days of perfectly planned productivity, and because we associate feeling productive with completed lists, it can be hard to feel productive at the end of the day. We need to retrain our brains to associate the feeling of accomplishment with diligence, with using time well, *not* with checking tasks off a list (although a list is a helpful tool to encourage and track diligent work). This is not just a different scale of productivity; it's an entirely different system. You can be just as productive as anyone else because you can use your time just as well as they use theirs, regardless of how many hours of focused work they are able to do in a day.

But why is it important that we shift from trying to get things done to trying to use time well? The two sound like almost the same thing, but there are four ways that changing your focus can change you.

Focusing on using time well gives you a positive attitude toward the work of motherhood. When you are trying your best to get things done, your children feel like an interruption to your "real work." Whether they are behaving well or being naughty, they get in the way of checking off the next task, and it is easy to resent them when the next task is your main goal. But when your priority is to use time well, then spending time on your children is not an interruption but is often the best way you can use your time. And when it comes to the mundane tasks that never stay done? They can seem useless and annoying when you want to get things done. But they feel meaningful when you want to use time well because they obviously must be done. Is there a dirty diaper? Then the best use of your time is to change it. Is there a traffic jam on the way to the grocery store? Then the best use of your time is to sit patiently in that traffic jam. What used to be inconveniences are now your real work. Instead of blaming them for how little you get done, they become a part of how well you used your time. And naptime? Naptime is never long enough to accomplish everything you want to do. But it's always long enough to use every minute of it well, whether for work or for rest.

Focusing on using time well helps you get the right tasks done. Imagine a minister who spent a day organizing his entire office. He got a lot done, right? But what if organizing his office was his way of avoiding the pain of visiting a couple who had just lost their baby? He may have gotten a lot done, but he didn't use his time well. There are days I do the same. I may check fifteen tasks off my list, but if I do that at the expense of reading the Bible to my daughter, disciplining her, or cuddling with her before bed, what did I really accomplish? I got a lot done, but I didn't make the best use of my time because I didn't do the right tasks. I didn't contribute to my goal of the salvation and sanctification of my family.

Focusing on using time well helps you feel more productive. This is possible because your focus is on the effort you put into your day, which you can control, instead of the results you get out of your day, which you cannot control. If your child is sick, for example, what you get out of your day is probably not a long list of completed tasks, but you can still feel productive because what you put into your day—your effort in comforting and caring for your child—was the best possible use of your time. This means that even as a mom, you can feel productive every day.

You can have high expectations for the way you spend your time; just don't make them exact expectations. Expect diligence of yourself because that is what God commands, but don't expect to get a specific number of tasks done. Motherhood can easily ruin exact expectations; it cannot touch high ones.

Focusing on using time well helps you rest better. When you focus only on getting things done, the tendency is to reward yourself every time you complete a task. This type of rest is reactive. It says, "I'm working so hard, and I'm so stressed. My kids are yelling. I need an escape. I deserve this." It tends to rely on food and entertainment instead of on God and leaves you feeling even more restless. When you focus on using time well, however, you are more likely to rest in a way that truly rejuvenates you. You are also more likely to put in the work required to make the rest effective. Yes, rest is a gift of God and is often the best use of your time, but it is usually most beneficial when it comes *after* you have done your work. Sometimes restlessness comes not from a lack of breaks but from a lack of putting energy into work. Even God rested *after* creation, not before or during. Resting when you have not done the work is like eating when you are not hungry; it's simply not as satisfying. If you work hard when it's time to work, you can rest easy when it's time to rest.

So how can you move your focus from getting things done to using time well? Simply by asking this question every time you are trying to decide what to do next: What is the best use of my time right now? Better yet, turn the question into a prayer: God, what is the best use of my time right now? Your answer could be cuddling with your child, responding to email, kissing your husband, opening your Bible, tackling the next task on your list, or making a cup of coffee. Often the answer comes naturally—a meal must be cooked or a mess must be cleaned up. At other times, though, the answer isn't obvious. Maybe it's naptime and your house is a mess, your email inbox is overflowing, and you feel like you haven't had a mental break in two days. What is the best use of your time then?

The easiest way to answer the question is with a calendar, a routine, and a to-do list.[4] These are tools that make it almost automatic to figure out how best to use your time. The calendar lists events, letting you know what must happen today. The routine lists

---

4. Resources I have found helpful on how to set up and manage these tools include Phylicia Masonheimer, "How to Create a Daily Routine (Tutorial)," *Phylicia Masonheimer* (blog), January 27, 2016, http://phyliciadelta.com/daily-routine-new-baby/; Matt Perman, *What's Best Next: How the Gospel Transforms the Way You Get Things Done* (Grand Rapids: Zondervan, 2016); Tim Challies, *Do More Better: A Practical Guide to Productivity* (Minneapolis: Cruciform Press, 2015); and David Allen, *Getting Things Done: The Art of Stress-Free Productivity* (London: Piatkus, 2015). Reading about other people's methods can be helpful, but keep in mind that they have probably taken years to develop methods that work for the way *they* think. Experiment with their methods, but keep only what works for you and tweak it so that it fits the way you think.

tasks that need to be done over and over, letting you know what should be done today in order to keep up with your responsibilities. The to-do list lists tasks that need to be done once, letting you know what you can do today if you have extra time. The purpose of these tools is not to stick to them pharisaically or to base your worth on them. No, their purpose is to help you do Martha work with a Mary mind-set.

Like Martha, you have much serving to do, but unlike Martha, you don't have to be distracted, anxious, and troubled while you do it. You can feel less distracted by using a calendar, routine, and to-do list to free your mind from trying to remember all the details. The feeling that comes from knowing events and tasks are written down instead of pinging around in your mind is life-changing. You can feel less anxious by using these tools to define what "done" means for today—not every task is checked off but the work that should have been done today did indeed get done. And you can feel less troubled by using these tools to have the confidence that you are doing the right task at the right time. Take the time to learn how these tools work best for your personality and your family so that you, like Mary, can focus on the one thing needful without neglecting the work God has set before you.

GROW IN SANCTIFICATION

Just as getting things done is not God's command to you, neither is it His will for you. When you let your two-year-old help unload silverware from the dishwasher, your purpose is not to get the silverware unloaded quickly. If it were, it would be more efficient to do it yourself. Your purpose is to train her for something more. You want her to be a willing worker now so that she will be a willing worker later.

When God puts tasks in front of you like washing clothes, cleaning bathrooms, and wiping faces, do you think His only purpose is for you to clean clothes, bathrooms, and faces? God is so creative and purposeful. He created bees that perform intricate dances to show the other bees where to find pollen. He created stars and gravity and a way for the earth to rotate on its axis and orbit the sun. Do you really think He couldn't get the floor vacuumed or the food prepared without you? Do you think He couldn't have thought of a more "efficient" way to raise children? If He could easily get this work done in other ways but still chooses to use you, He *must* have a bigger purpose.

So what is His purpose? Why give you bathrooms to clean and baskets of laundry to empty? Certainly not as a means to happiness or fulfillment for you. If being happy depended on a clean bathroom, it wouldn't last a day. If fulfillment was found in an empty laundry basket, it wouldn't last a minute. No, if you are a child of God, His will for you is not merely to get things done. His will for you is sanctification (1 Thess. 4:3). Your work is a tool He uses to produce the fruit of the Spirit in you to make you more like Christ (Gal. 5:22–23).

The tasks God has set before you are the best ones you can do to grow in sanctification. J. R. Miller writes,

> You pray to have the Christian graces in your life. You want to have joy, patience, gentleness, humility, mercifulness. But these heavenly qualities cannot be put into your life at once; they have to grow from small beginnings to perfection—"first the blade, then the ear, then the full grain in the ear,"—and that requires a long time.[5]

God grows the fruit of the Spirit in you by giving you opportunities to act in ways that are loving, joyful, patient, kind, good, faithful, gentle, or self-controlled. To do His will, then, is to use the power of the Holy Spirit within you to take those opportunities, many of which are your basic tasks and most of which go against your natural human will. Think about how your work as a mother and homemaker relates to what God wants you to be.

God wants you to be loving. My mom is the most selfless person I know. She would do anything

5. J. R. Miller, *The Beauty of Self-Control* (New York: Thomas Y. Crowell, 1911), 193.

for anyone at any moment. When I became a mom, I began to realize why. Lives literally depended on her selfless love, and after decades of practicing that love, pouring it out became habitual and almost automatic. What better way to learn love than to care for a tiny, helpless, needy human that not only grew inside your body but can even receive food from your body?

God wants you to be joyful. There are only two ways to have joy. You must either get everything you want, or you must train your mind to be joyful regardless of whether you get what you want or not. The first is impossible for most of us; the second is the only way to live. What better way to learn joy than to deny yourself so habitually for the sake of another person that your joy no longer depends on your own wants and needs?

God wants you to be patient. Moms put in long hours and wait years to see results. What better way to learn patience than to practice it daily, even hourly, by waiting on and reasoning with tiny people who are in no hurry and do not have fully developed minds?

God wants you to be kind. What better way to learn kindness than to be in charge of the daily training of a child in whom you see so much of your own sin and unkindness?

God wants you to be good. What better way to learn goodness than to have someone watching and learning from your every word and action?

God wants you to be faithful. What better way to learn faithfulness than to be required to work long hours at a job with no pay, no recognition, and no possibility of promotion?

God wants you to be gentle. What better way to learn gentleness than to be given the responsibility of caring physically for a fragile newborn and emotionally for a tender heart?

God wants you to be self-controlled. What better way to learn self-control than to be required to complete dirty, mundane tasks over and over, day after day?

Let's narrow the focus to just one of these fruits—self-control—to see how we can use it as motivation in our work. Self-control, or self-discipline, is a common topic in the Bible. Proverbs says someone without self-control is like a city whose walls are broken (25:28), and someone with it is more powerful than the conqueror of a city (16:32). Paul writes to Timothy that God has given us a spirit of self-control (2 Tim. 1:7). Peter tells us that self-control is one of the qualities that keeps us from being ineffective or unfruitful in the knowledge of Jesus (2 Peter 1:8). We can tell God wants us to grow in self-control, but how?

Do you remember filling out penmanship worksheets in elementary school? Did you save those worksheets? Maybe a few, if you were proud of your handwriting. But the point of the exercise was not the worksheets themselves. It was to master the basics of writing, to make forming letters so habitual that you could write without even thinking about how each letter is made. Without mastering the basics of a skill through practice, you will never be able to do greater things with that skill.

If you never master basic self-control by practicing and making it a habit in little things, it will be hard to have self-control in greater things when they come along. You don't know what difficult temptation, circumstance, or work God has for you in the future. But no matter what comes, it will be easier if you have practiced self-control in the meantime.

So what are the little things in your life right now that will give you practice? Sticking with a cleaning routine? Limiting social media? Eating healthier meals? These things aren't necessarily a choice between something sinful and something holy, and they certainly aren't a way to earn salvation, but they are ways to practice self-control and to develop assurance that the Holy Spirit *is* present and working His fruit in your heart.

Your spiritual life is so tightly intertwined with everything else that practicing self-control in areas like these will make a difference in whether you are becoming more like Christ or not. Just like every bite of food becomes a part of your physical body, so every choice becomes a part of who you are spiritually. One bite of chocolate doesn't make an obvious difference to your body (thankfully!), but a bite of chocolate every time you walk through the kitchen for a month will certainly show up at the end of the month. A choice of what you shouldn't be doing with your time over what you should be doing doesn't instantly derail your spiritual life, but consistently making "small" wrong choices will have an impact. Should you be spending time talking with your children or your husband? Then washing dishes makes you slightly less like Christ. Should you be doing your devotions? Then scrolling through your phone makes you slightly less like Him. C. S. Lewis said,

> Every time you make a choice you are turning the central part of you, the part of you that chooses, into something a little different than it was before. And taking your life as a whole, with all your innumerable choices, all your life long you are slowly turning this central thing into a heavenly creature or a hellish creature.... Each of us at each moment is progressing to the one state or the other.[6]

When I think about it this way, it becomes easier, by the Spirit's power, to willingly make the choice to do the mundane work. Jesus was obedient to the point of death (Phil. 2:8). Can't I be obedient to the point of scrubbing the shower? If that's what I have to do in this moment to become more like Christ, then I will scrub that shower with joy!

And the choices start today. When I see a fit person jogging, I'd like to think she's jogging because

---

6. C. S. Lewis, *Mere Christianity* (New York: Macmillan, 1952), 56.

she's fit. That would give me an excuse not to jog until I'm fit. But I know that's backward. She's fit because she exercises regularly and eats well. If I exercised regularly and stopped eating chocolate chips, I would have similar results.

In the same way, we like to think people who are diligent in the work God gives them are naturally self-controlled. That would give us an excuse by allowing us to claim we "just aren't that disciplined." But that's backward. People are self-controlled because they have consistently put in the hard work, even when they don't feel like it. Blogger Lisa Hensley writes, "Feelings follow action," and fruits of the Spirit follow obedience.

How does someone become fit? By doing what a fit person would do. How can you grow in self-control? By doing what a self-controlled person would do. If I were a self-controlled person, I would clean my bathrooms every Thursday morning—not because they can't wait until Friday but because I want to practice self-control. The fact that the bathrooms are clean by the time I'm done practicing self-control is just a bonus.

Sometimes it takes more self-control not to clean the bathrooms. When a friend needs your time, maybe setting your to-do list aside makes you more like Christ. Sometimes it requires focusing on other fruits of the Spirit to get the job done. Maybe love, not self-control, helps you pack your husband's lunches. Maybe gentleness helps you hold your teething baby with tenderness when you just want to be by yourself. The way the fruits influence your work will depend greatly on your personal strengths and weaknesses.

Progressing in sanctification by the Spirit's power helps you be and feel more productive because you are more focused on the horizon of eternity and because fruits like self-control help a person get more done. After all, there really is no such thing as time management. You have twenty-four hours in the day, just like everyone else, and you can't manage time so that you get more hours. You can manage only yourself within those hours. Self-control is the greatest productivity hack there is. There's no method or system that bypasses it or makes it unnecessary. It can't be taught; it can only be practiced—when we feel like practicing and when we don't.

Do you see how this changes your work? You no longer feel the need to give up on patience and joy in order to have a productive day. Instead, the Spirit living in you works the fruit that motivates you to use your time well. Sometimes the list will get done, and sometimes it won't. But thank God that His will is so much greater than your list. It's not about the laundry anymore. It's not about the countertops, the diapers, the crumbs. It's about being like Christ! And that is permanent work that cannot be undone like the room you just tidied. Yes, your work on earth can be boring, messy, and inefficient. There's a reason movies put the hard work into montages backed with uplifting music. Nobody wants to see all the work that is required to reach a happy ending.

Sometimes I don't want to see the work either. If it were up to me, I would have chosen a more glamorous way to take up the cross daily. But this is my work, given to me by my God, included in the things He says will work together for my good (Rom. 8:28). What does He mean by "my good"? Not monetary gain, not praise for me, not kids who "turn out good," not even a full-circle story in which I go through hard times but come out victorious before I die. No, "my good" is that I be conformed to the image of Christ by the power of the Spirit (Rom. 8:29), and God will put into my life exactly what is needed for that to happen. His thoughts, ways, and will are far above mine, and I trust that what He says is truth. I trust that my victory, my happy ending, will come after I die because Jesus Christ died for me.

GLORIFY GOD

God did not create your mind in a way that allows you to find fulfillment in getting things done; that's not your purpose. You may have a sense of satisfaction in getting things done, but it will not last, because productivity was never meant to be the source of your satisfaction. To focus solely on getting things done is to try to get glory for yourself. But God created you for the purpose of giving glory to Him, and you cannot find fulfillment in trying to follow a path other than the one set forth by the Creator of your mind.

In His divine wisdom, God commanded Adam to tend the garden of Eden because Adam's obedience brought God glory, not because God couldn't get it done on His own. God gave Adam a sense of fulfillment when the work was accomplished not because the work itself was the point but because in doing the work, he was obeying and glorifying God.

God has given you work too. You have a home, a family, and other responsibilities. He has called you to motherhood, and in order to obey Him, you must faithfully do the work He has set before you. In doing that work you will be productive for the sake of God's glory, not for the sake of productivity. And when you are productive, God will give you a sense of accomplishment—not because you were productive in the world's eyes, but because you were obedient in God's eyes.

This goes against everything that society and human nature have ingrained in our minds. We think that work can fulfill us and that if it doesn't, we must have chosen the wrong job. We think that motherhood can fulfill us and that if it doesn't, we must be doing something wrong. But motherhood will not fulfill you because it was not meant to. It will empty you, and that is how it is supposed to be. Just look at Jesus's example. If anyone deserved to be fulfilled, it was He. But "instead of trying to fulfill

Himself, Jesus 'emptied himself,'"[7] and He did it by taking "upon him the form of a servant" (Phil. 2:7).

People often ask what you would do if you had only twenty-four hours left to live. We don't have to wonder what Jesus would do in that situation because it is recorded for us in the Bible. He would take the form of a servant by washing the feet of those He was influencing, by serving them a meal, and by pouring out His life on the cross for them. Elisabeth Eliot observes, "Does God ask us to do what is beneath us? This question will never trouble us again if we consider the Lord of heaven taking a towel and washing feet."[8] When we think about what Jesus did for us, the least we can do is pour out our energy, time, and desires for those He has called us to influence.

If you pour yourself out, God will refill you. If you attempt to fill yourself up, God will make it clear that you cannot. But how does God refill you? He doesn't fill a tank in your brain while you're sleeping. Instead, He tells you to read His Word, to pray, and to have fellowship with His people. If you have been emptied and don't feel refilled, persevere in these three instructions.

Read the Word. Consistency is key, and daily time in the Word is best. The only way to set your mind on

---

7. Hannah Anderson, *Humble Roots: How Humility Grounds and Nourishes Your Soul* (Chicago: Moody, 2016), 74.

8. Elliot, *Discipline*, 122.

things above (Col. 3:2) is to soak your mind in the Word from above. The thoughts that come from your mind reflect the information you are putting into it. What better information to fill your mind with than God's information? When you start reading the Bible every day, you probably will not feel like a different person immediately. But persevere, and when you look back after a year, you will see that the Spirit has worked through the Word, as promised (2 Tim. 3:16–17). He will reward you if you humbly seek Him (Heb. 11:6).

Make prayer your initial response to both the stressful and the wonderful moments of motherhood. How can you expect the peace of God to guard your mind (Phil. 4:7) if your mind is not focused on God for much of the day? Part of why motherhood is so sanctifying is that there are moments so stressful that you cannot help but go to God. Nothing else can provide a solution or even a distraction. You feel helpless, and your last-ditch effort is exactly what your first effort should be in any situation—desperate prayer to God. Motherhood also brings moments that are so wonderful you can't help but praise God. One stands out for me from the hazy weeks just after my daughter was born. I had been up most of the night with her on my chest, and all of a sudden when I looked down at her sleeping so peacefully, looking so beautiful, I began sobbing out of gratitude to God that He had handpicked her for me and me for her.

And shouldn't our lives be filled with moments like these? Shouldn't we allow ourselves to be swept away with emotion because we are grateful to God, who created love and is love and placed these tiny, precious gifts into our lives? When we focus solely on productivity and lists, we miss out on so much gratitude, so much communion with God, because we forget to notice the beautiful moments, and we think that we can solve our problems by making small adjustments to our schedules or by making another list. No, bring it all to God first. Let prayer be your first response every time. Practice it over and over throughout the day. The beauty of practicing prayer is that the practice is prayer. Just pray. Without ceasing.

Seek out communion with God's people. There are three types of people you should be spending time with—those further along in life for their wisdom, those at a similar stage in life for their practical advice, and those behind you in life to pass along the wisdom God has given you. For a long time, I saw people I admired from a distance in all three of these groups, and I wished I could be friends with them and learn from them. I'm slowly learning that the way to be friends with people you want to be friends with is to initiate a friendship. Text them to ask if they want to get coffee. Walk over and say hi, even if you don't know what you'll say next. As a new mom, you need as much wisdom from the godly people in your life (not only from the internet) as you can get, and to get it, you need to ask for it. Even asking the simple question, "What is your best piece of parenting advice?" might bring out some gem they have learned after years or decades of parenting. Pray to God for wisdom, but don't forget that He often gives it through the wise, godly people in your life.

When you are being emptied and refilled daily, it is time to strive for contentment. One way my daughter "glorifies" me as her mother is by accepting what I give her—food, toys, affection—and by being happy with it and grateful for it. When she is content, she makes me look like a good mom. When she is not, well, we've all had meltdowns in the grocery store. Her discontent makes people think less highly of me.

When we are happy with the gifts God has given us, we witness to the world that He is a good God. This glorifies Him. When we are not content with what He has given us, we witness to the world that we think He is not a good God, that He does not have the best interests of His people in mind, and that we don't trust Him to make us happy.

Satan uses this issue of contentment to try to take God's glory away. One of his strategies today is this: put a generation of women in a world that tells them they can and should be able to get anything they want at any time. Then make them mothers—a role that daily requires them to give up things they want for the good of someone else.

But contentment is not some magical dust God sprinkles over you. It's not a destination to reach and stay at. It must be learned and fought for. Even Paul had to learn it (Phil. 4:11)! So how can you combat Satan's strategy and glorify God? By fighting for contentment in the role God has called you to, by the power of the Holy Spirit. How can you do that?

Believe what God says about Himself. He says He is good (Pss. 119:68; 145:9). He says that if you love Him and are called according to His purpose, everything in your life works together for good (Rom. 8:28). Do you believe this? If you do, then you must also believe that any command He gives is for your good. Among many other commands, He tells you to work heartily (Col. 3:23). He would not tell you this if the work in front of you was not good for you. Even if it feels small or boring at times, you can grow in contentment by repeating these truths to yourself again and again.

Work heartily, as for the Lord and not for men (Col. 3:23). Doing your work with energy makes it go by faster and helps you feel energized by it rather than depleted. The exhaustion that comes at the end of a day of hard work is a far better feeling than the tiredness at the end of a lazy day of short tasks sandwiched between long breaks on social media. It is laziness that breeds discontent, not work. And while work does not guarantee contentment, you will never be content if you don't do the work the Lord has put in front of you. It is in obedience that you find peace.

Remember your reward. Read on in Colossians 3: Work "heartily…knowing that of the Lord ye shall receive the reward of the inheritance" (vv. 23–24). God Himself gives the incentive of reward, and it's not wrong to look forward to it. No matter what you do, knowing there is a reward waiting for you at the end is a wonderful incentive. As Paul wrote, "For I reckon that the sufferings of this present time are not worthy to be compared with the glory which shall be revealed in us" (Rom. 8:18).

Learn to love your work. If a task must be done, you might as well learn to love it. You can learn to love it in the same way that someone can learn to love investing five dollars in a retirement account instead of spending it at Chick-fil-A—by focusing on the long-term results rather than on the immediate satisfaction. And isn't that what so much of the Christian walk is about? We must learn to deny what our flesh wants in the moment, which leads to death, in order to do what God wills by the Spirit's power, which is life (Rom. 8:13).

Realize that the work of motherhood and homemaking must be learned. We tend to think that it's a natural role and must therefore come easily, but it doesn't.

We know how to do many of the individual tasks, but putting them all together in a way that gets it all done is hard and takes time to figure out. But just like any other job, you don't have to start out as an expert. You can search out people in person or online to teach you better ways of doing the work. You can improve with time. Blogger Lara Casey points out, "Little by little, progress adds up."[9] As your kids grow, so do you.

Get good at your work. What activities do you enjoy doing? What activities are you good at? The two lists are probably similar. A reasonable conclusion is that if you want to like an activity or task more, you need to get better at it. How can you get better at your work? By practice. How can you practice? By doing it over and over—weekly, daily, or hourly. How convenient that motherhood and homemaking put you in a position that requires you to do just that. If you put in the effort, you can't help but get better at your work and therefore learn to enjoy it more.

Use your particular gifts. Are you naturally organized? Creative? Thrifty? Make your work about the gifts God has given you, and you will be more content—both with the work and with your gifts. I disliked

---

9. Lara Casey, "Little by Little: Progress Not Perfection," *Lara Casey.com* (blog), January 27, 2016, http://laracasey.com/2017/01/27/progress-not-perfection/.

grocery shopping until I made it all about planning and efficiency, two things that I love. Now I like grocery shopping. How can you apply the same tactic? Are you good at finding great deals? Make it about finding the best deal. Are you creative? Make it about finding unique ingredients. As Mary Poppins sings,

> In every job that must be done
> There is an element of fun.
> You find the fun and snap!
> The job's a game.

Accept what you can accomplish in a day. Productivity is like money in that you tend to think that if you had just a little more, you would be happy. You won't. When you get more, you'll want more. You must be aware of how much you can and should accomplish in a day and you must work hard, but you must also train your mind to be content with what was accomplished. God has the hairs on your head numbered (Luke 12:7). Do you think He didn't number the crumbs that fell from the high chair today? Do you think He didn't plan the fights you had to mediate, the tears you had to wipe? He planned those "interruptions," and He planned them for your good. They did not get in the way of your "real work." Because He planned them, they *were* your real work. They *were* your calling. Contentment doesn't just apply to whether you are happy with your body or your clothes. God gave you a limited and specific level of ability, time, and opportunity to get things done.

You must use time and talents well, but when you have done that, you *must* be content with what you accomplished, because it is what God meant for you to accomplish.

Don't compare productivity levels. If you focus on how your mom friend can do more in a day than you could ever dream of doing, you will feel defeated. If you focus on how she can't do as much, you will feel proud. Either result is sinful. Instead, remember that you don't know her whole story. Just as God created different people with different types and levels of intelligence, so He created us with varied capacity and opportunity for productivity. You may lack in "housekeeping productivity" but excel in "hospitality productivity," and your friend may be the opposite. The solution is to stop looking around at others and simply look to God for help to use *your* time and talents well, and then offer encouragement to others to do the same.

Fight for contentment daily. If you struggle with discontent, try to pinpoint what is causing it. On the one hand, is it something that you can and should be working on or changing? Then work at it. Spiritual life is so intertwined with your physical life and environment that often tackling a project or goal you should have finished months ago can help in the fight for contentment. It's not the finished goal that will make you content, but it is God's will that you care for the blessings and do the work He has placed in front of you, and you cannot expect contentment outside that will. On the other hand, is your struggle with discontent over something that you cannot or should not be working on or changing? Then soak your mind in the Word of God, prayer, and good books and podcasts so that it is not being soaked in the matter of discontent. No one stays content without prayer, work, and the power of the Holy Spirit.

Practice gratitude. Pray thanksgiving and sing praises all day long, every time you think to do so. It will change your experience of motherhood and of life. It is what God created you for. You are included in "the people…I formed for myself; they shall shew forth my praise" (Isa. 43:21). It doesn't matter how productive you may be in the world's eyes. If you shirk the purpose for which God made you, productivity means nothing and you will never feel satisfied, no matter how much you strive for it. If, however, you strive for productivity not as a means to prop yourself up but as a tool to bring glory to God, you can be *and* feel productive.

CONCLUSION

Maybe you, like me, have spent years assuming that getting things done is God's call to you, God's will for you, and God's purpose in creating you. It's freeing to realize this is not true, but the fight to change your mind-set is not over. You must continually remind yourself of truth.

When your children seem to be getting in the way of your work, remind yourself that God's call to you is not to get things done but to use time well, and then do whatever is the best use of your time in that moment.

When your tasks seem mundane, remind yourself that God's will for you is not to get things done but to grow in sanctification, and then focus on how each task done for God is making you more like Christ.

When your goals and dreams seem to be on hold, remind yourself that God's purpose for you is not to get things done but to glorify Him, and then empty yourself willingly, grasping His promise that His burden is easy, resting content in knowing that one day you will see with your own eyes how He has worked everything together for your good and His glory.

If you forget all this, you are like a carpenter who forgets that he is building a house for his family and starts obsessing over how many nails he can pound in each day. Yes, he needs to pound in nails in order to build the house, but the nails are not the point of what he is doing. You too are building, but you're working on a kingdom. All your actions, all your choices, all the things you do or leave undone are either furthering or hindering this kingdom. Many tasks must be completed for this kingdom to come, but the tasks themselves are not the point of what you are doing.

When the carpenter focuses instead on the love and laughter his family will one day share in the house he is building, he doesn't think much of the nails, and yet he pounds more in and appreciates them more because he realizes what they are helping him build. When you focus on the coming kingdom of God and the joy and glory you'll share with your extended Christian family in heaven, your need to feel productive will fade to the background, and yet you will be and feel more productive because you have a far greater purpose. There's no need to obsess over how many nails get pounded in today. We're participating in building God's kingdom, and it's the kingdom that matters.